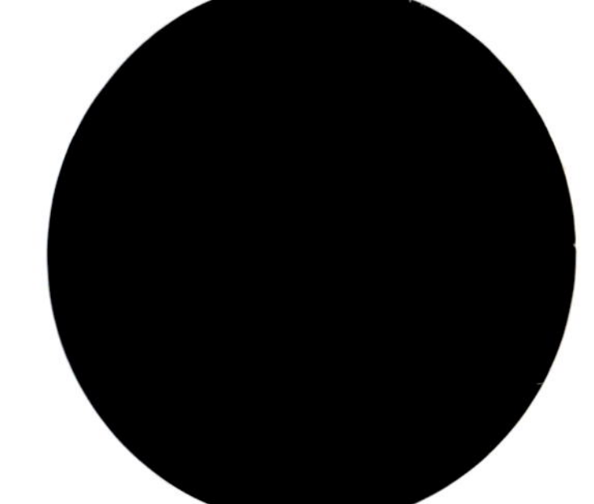

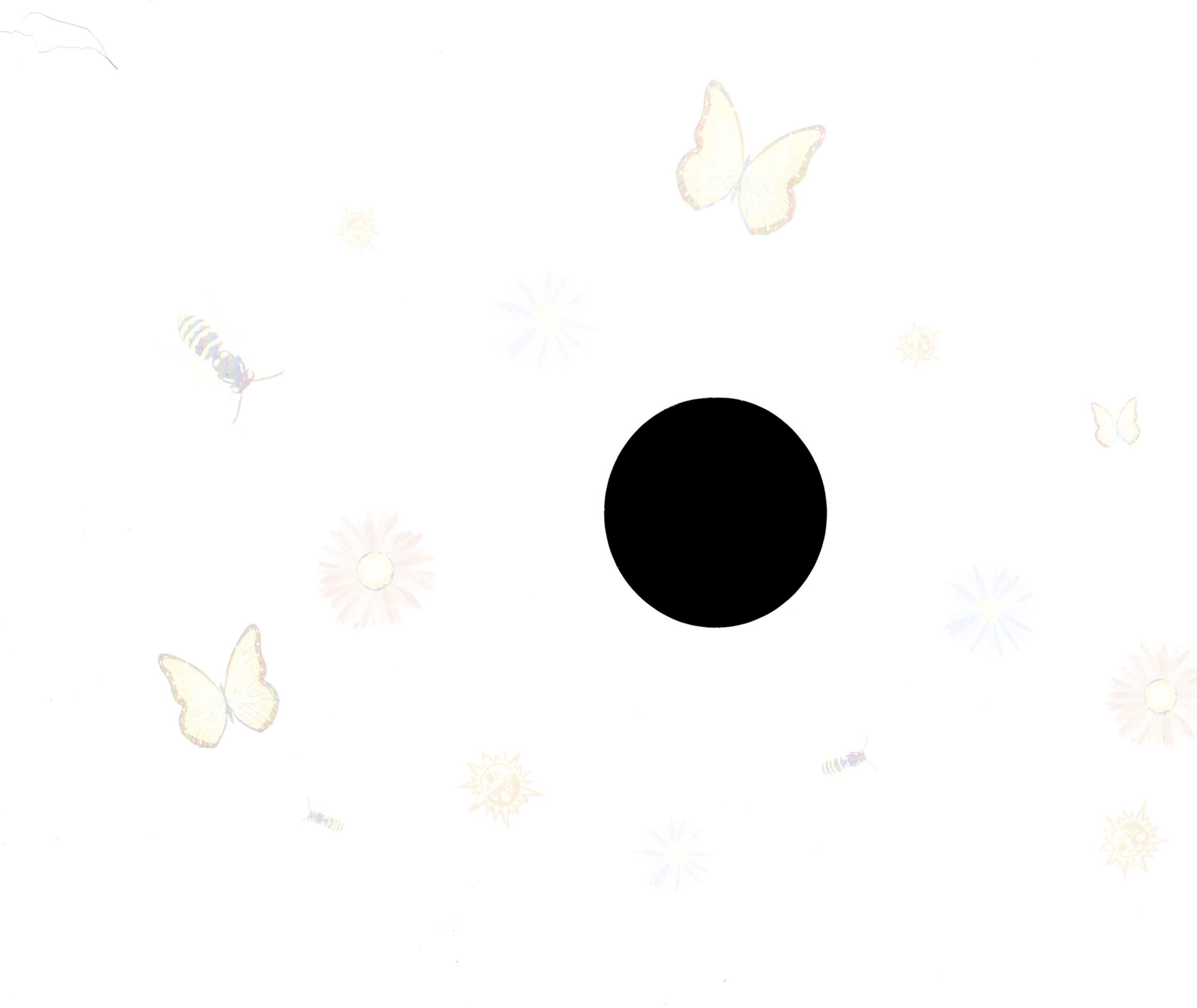

# Daisies

## Shall we ...

collect some common flowers, such as daisies, to create potions and perfumes. Collect some grass and make some pretend soup. Sing a song as we dance in the rose petals.

Find some interesting bottles to put the potions in. Make a funnel from a rolled up leaf. Lie down and look closely at all the daisies on the grass. Count how many daisies you can see.

Pick a few to make a daisy chain. Make a daisy bracelet with bark, or grass. Search for different sticks to mash or stir your potion.

Pull the daisy petals off one at a time and together count how many there are. Float some on the surface of a bowl of water.

# Beach Shadows

**Shall we ...**

Kick our shoes off and run on the beach. Sit in the soft wet sand and make a sand sculpture. Leap from shadow to shadow. Find the smallest shadow from the tiniest rock.

Draw around the shadow in the sand and see how it moves over the day. Create sculptures with driftwood to make a shadow picture.

Look for strange designs in the driftwood. Find the smoothest piece, a piece like a fish, a blob a thing. Make a line of driftwood and see if the sea can reach it.

Watch the sea play with driftwood and keep bringing it back to us. Use a potato peeler and carve some shapes into driftwood.

Create a giant shadow on the sand, with sheets and wood.  Look for bits of driftwood with holes to look through.

# Rolling

Shall we ...

roll some corn stem around your fingers. Watch the farmers as they cut the corn and roll the bales. Pick some stubble corn and roll a shape.

Use the old stubble to make some spiky shapes that don't roll. Search for a stone to roll along the ground. Watch as the wind rolls leaves around.

Make some bread that uses the flour that came from the corn. Roll the dough into shapes. Roll on the grass. Make a roll of old leaves.

Roll a small piece of damp soil and try to make a ball. Roll some home made 'soil clay' into a shape. Find some objects to roll down some tubes, or along two sticks.

Watch as the water in the stream rolls the leaves over and over at the bottom of a waterfall. Roll a slice of wood down a hill, try and catch it again.

Roll large and small pebbles down the slope and see which goes faster. Roll a leaf around your finger, pull it off carefully to make a little tunnel.

Carefully roll a stone along the sand to make a windy track. Curl ourselves up into a little ball and then slowly unroll again.

# Pebbles and rocks

**Shall we ...**

find a rock to sit on, walk on, stand on, hide behind. Play 1 2 3 where are you? Find different pebbles with lovely colours, patterns and textures

Have a look underneath and then put it back because it is someone's home. Take a torch and peer down through the gaps in the rock.

Stand on top of a rock and look down from on high to see our area in a different way. Draw on them with water. Make a picture using the pebbles.

Dip half in water and make a dark and light rock pattern. Balance them in an arc. Line them up from large to small.

Balance rocks on top of each other to make a tower. Make a stone table with large rocks and use little stones for plates.

Make a shape with pebbles and dance in it. Find the perfect rock to make a big splash in the shallow water. Climb up a big rock in our bare feet.

# Fruit

Shall we ...

go to a place where the strawberries grow. Search under the leaves to find the places the strawberries are hiding. Pick some and put them in our baskets and tubs.

Make jam, or a jelly or a smoothie. Wash it and eat it outside. Look inside to see if there is a space. Squash it and make strawberry juice. Count how many bites it takes to eat a strawberry.

Make a berry desert with layers of fruit and yoghurt. Melt a few chocolate buttons and dip the fruit in. Make our own gardening patch.

Plant a strawberry tower and keep it on the windowsill. Slice our fruit and make a salad with 5 different kinds of fruit. Go to the market and talk about all the fruit we can see.

Buy a new fruit to try. Plant the seed from the apple core and see if it grows. Make a chart to help us to remember to eat lots of fruit.

# Grasses

## Shall we ...

go for a walk and look for signs. Take a picnic and find a secret den in the tallest grass. Go for a walk in the grass.

Sing the song of Going on a Bearhunt as we go through the swishy, swashy grass. Look for as many different grasses as we can see.

Make teeny posies from all the tiny seed heads and then throw them into the wind. Use the cut grass to make pretend house shapes in the garden.

Lie down in the grass and stare at the sky. Leap and bound through the grass. Roll down a grassy bank. Roll down a hill together. Weave and knot the long grass stems.

Blow across a long piece of grass to make a loud noise. Bend and twist grass to make funny shapes. Measure the grass to find the longest bit or the shortest bit.

Use hard grass stems to 'stitch' some leaves together.

# Reflections

## Shall we ...

Go for a walk and find some puddles and look at our reflections. Take a small mirror to the wood and use it to look above us. Sit by the lake and watch the reflection of the hills or the trees. Go to the park and look for the reflections of the ducks on the pond. Throw a pebble in the pool and watch as it breaks up the still water and breaks up the reflection. Count how long it takes for the water to go smooth again. Fill a bowl of water and make our own little pond. Use two plastic mirrors and see if we can see each other around the other side of a large tree. Take some old CD's outside and watch as the light reflects off in many different colours. Find a large thin plastic mirror to bend and flex to make plants and trees grow and shrink. Look closely at your reflection in the shallow water, can you make your noses touch. Blow a giant bubble and find your reflection in it. Look into a friend's eyes and see if you can see a tiny you reflected in them.

# Bees

## Shall we ...

Make a wooden house for bees, ladybirds, lacewings, and earwigs to live in. Make a house for each mini beast that is in our garden. Look at a book to find out what they want in a house. Run around the garden buzzing like a bee. Walk to the shop and look at the different types and colours of honey. Put some honey in a little pot for you to dribble onto your bread or biscuit. Make some honey sandwiches. Make a honey drink to drink at lunchtime. Buy some real honeycomb to look at the shapes the bees have made from wax. Get some beeswax and roll it to make a candle. Make something from the soft wax around the cheese. Try to find some pictures of all the different types of minibeasts and which plants they like to visit. Find the binoculars and watch the bees visiting the flowers. Look at a bee picture and see if you can see their pollen sacks on their legs. Take a magnifying glass and look closely at the bugs in the garden. Watch the bees go into the long trumpet of the foxglove. Look for yellow pollen dust in a flower. Look closely at the ladybird as it opens its wings ready to fly.

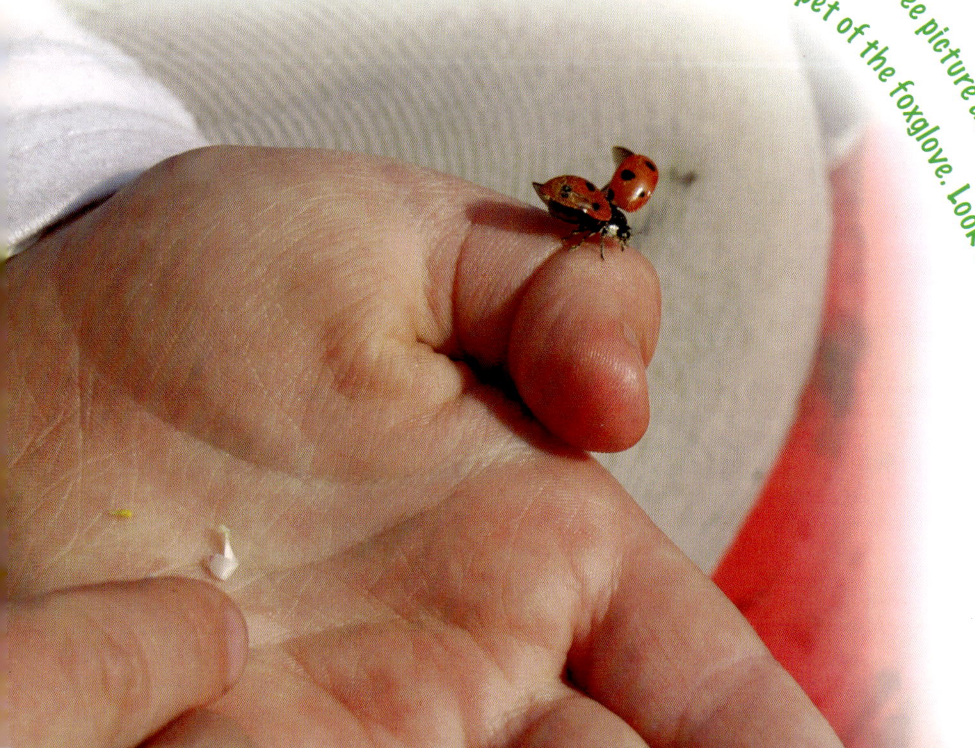